# Una competencia de ciencias

por Kama Einhorn
ilustrado por David Bergstein

**Scott Foresman**
is an imprint of

**PEARSON**

Glenview, Illinois • Boston, Massachusetts • Chandler, Arizona
Upper Saddle River, New Jersey

Every effort has been made to secure permission and provide appropriate credit for photographic material. The publisher deeply regrets any omission and pledges to correct errors called to its attention in subsequent editions.

Unless otherwise acknowledged, all photographs are the property of Pearson.

Photo locations denoted as follows: Top (T), Center (C), Bottom (B), Left (L), Right (R), Background (Bkgd)

Illustrations by David Bergstein

8(B) ®Roger Ressmeyer/Corbis

ISBN 13: 978-0-328-53413-5
ISBN 10:      0-328-53413-7

**Copyright © by Pearson Education, Inc., or its affiliates.** All rights reserved. Printed in the United States of America. This publication is protected by copyright, and permission should be obtained from the publisher prior to any prohibited reproduction, storage in a retrieval system, or transmission in any form or by any means, electronic, mechanical, photocopying, recording, or likewise. For information regarding permissions, write to Pearson Curriculum Rights & Permissions, One Lake Street, Upper Saddle River, New Jersey 07458.

**Pearson®** is a trademark, in the U.S. and/or other countries, of Pearson plc or its affiliates.

**Scott Foresman®** is a trademark, in the U.S. and/or other countries, of Pearson Education, Inc., or its affiliates.

2 3 4 5 6 7 8 9 10 V0N4 13 12 11 10

—Habrá una competencia de ciencias en nuestro pueblo —nos empezó a contar la profesora Grady—. Cada grado presentará un proyecto. Toda la clase trabajará en grupo. Mucha gente vendrá a ver la competencia.

—¿Qué creen que podemos hacer? —preguntó la profesora Grady.

—¡Hagamos un nuevo tipo de zapato! —dijo Tom.

—¡Estudiemos a los simios! —dijo Laura.

—Estamos estudiando los volcanes —dijo Gustavo—. ¿Por qué no hacemos la maqueta de un volcán?

—¡Palabras sabias! Mostraremos cómo erupciona un volcán —dijeron todos muy alegres.

Buscamos una botella vacía y la cubrimos con masa. Beto y Vero fueron llenando la botella con agua tibia y colorante rojo. Luego agregamos jabón y bicarbonato de soda.

Durante la competencia, le agregamos vinagre a nuestro volcán y ¡erupcionó! De la boca del volcán salió una espuma roja que parecía lava caliente rodando por las montañas.

¿Quién crees que ganó el primer premio? ¡Nosotros!

# Experimentos a diario

**Leamos juntos**

Los científicos de todo el mundo estudian y trabajan juntos en sus experimentos. El estudio de los volcanes nos ayuda a entender cómo se forman y erupcionan. También nos ayuda a identificar las señales que dan antes de erupcionar. Comprender esas señales puede salvar la vida de mucha gente que vive cerca de los volcanes. Todos los científicos hacen experimentos, ponen a prueba sus hipótesis y sacan conclusiones a partir de sus estudios.

**Estos científicos estudian mapas para ayudar a la gente antes de que los volcanes erupcionen.**

# The Story of Our Freedom

### by Leo Lamont

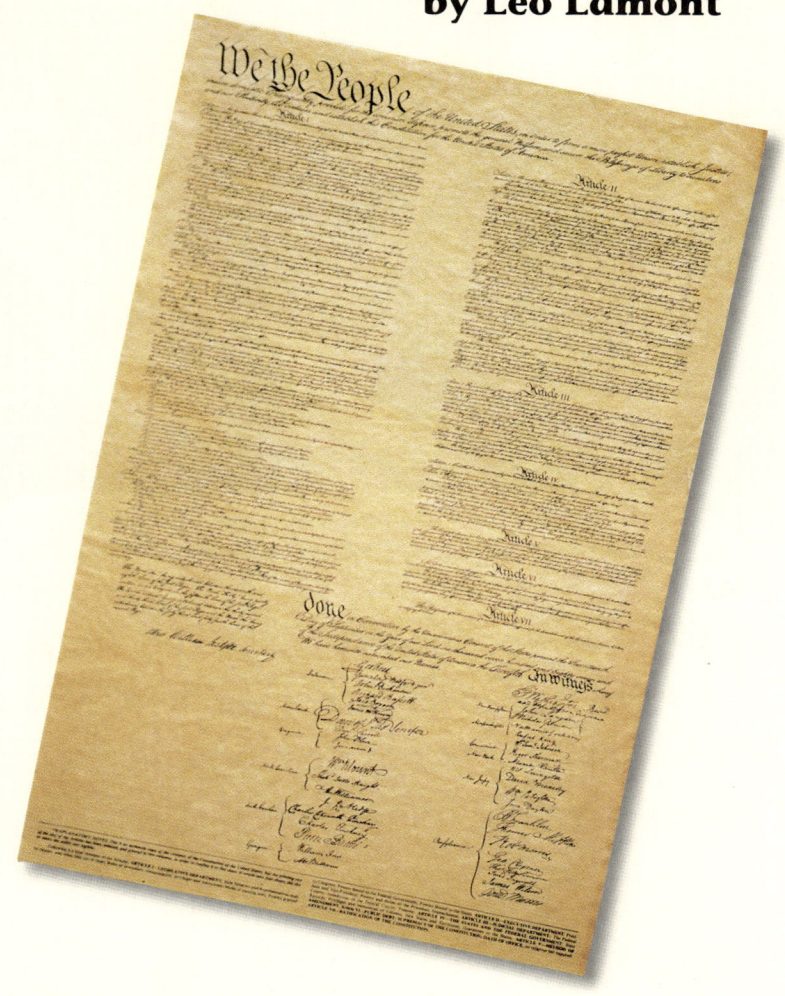

**PEARSON**

Glenview, Illinois • Boston, Massachusetts • Chandler, Arizona
Upper Saddle River, New Jersey

We are free to read what we want.

We have freedoms in the United States.
We are free to say what we think. We are free to write it. We are free to gather, or come together. We are free to vote.

People are free to gather.

    Not all countries have these freedoms. In some countries, people cannot gather. Laws, or rules, stop them from coming together. If people break the law, they get into trouble.

3

We have freedom to vote.

The government of the United States protects our freedoms. This means it keeps them safe.

Our government makes laws. The laws make sure we keep our rights.

This was the first flag of the United States.

Who made these laws? Why?
We have to learn about the beginning of the United States.

Our country was ruled by Great Britain until 1776.

Long ago, the United States was not a country. It was ruled by a king. The king was from Great Britain.

Many people did not want this. They wanted to rule themselves.

The Declaration of Independence

On July 4, 1776, our leaders wrote a paper. It was the Declaration of Independence. A declaration is an announcement. Independence means freedom.

July 4 is now a holiday in the United States.

The United States won in 1781.

The United States had to fight for freedom. The British king wanted land. After many years, the United States finally won.

The United States Constitution

Then, the United States started to plan a government.

In 1787, the leaders met. They wrote another paper. It was called the United States Constitution. A constitution tells about laws.

Leaders wrote the U.S. Constitution.

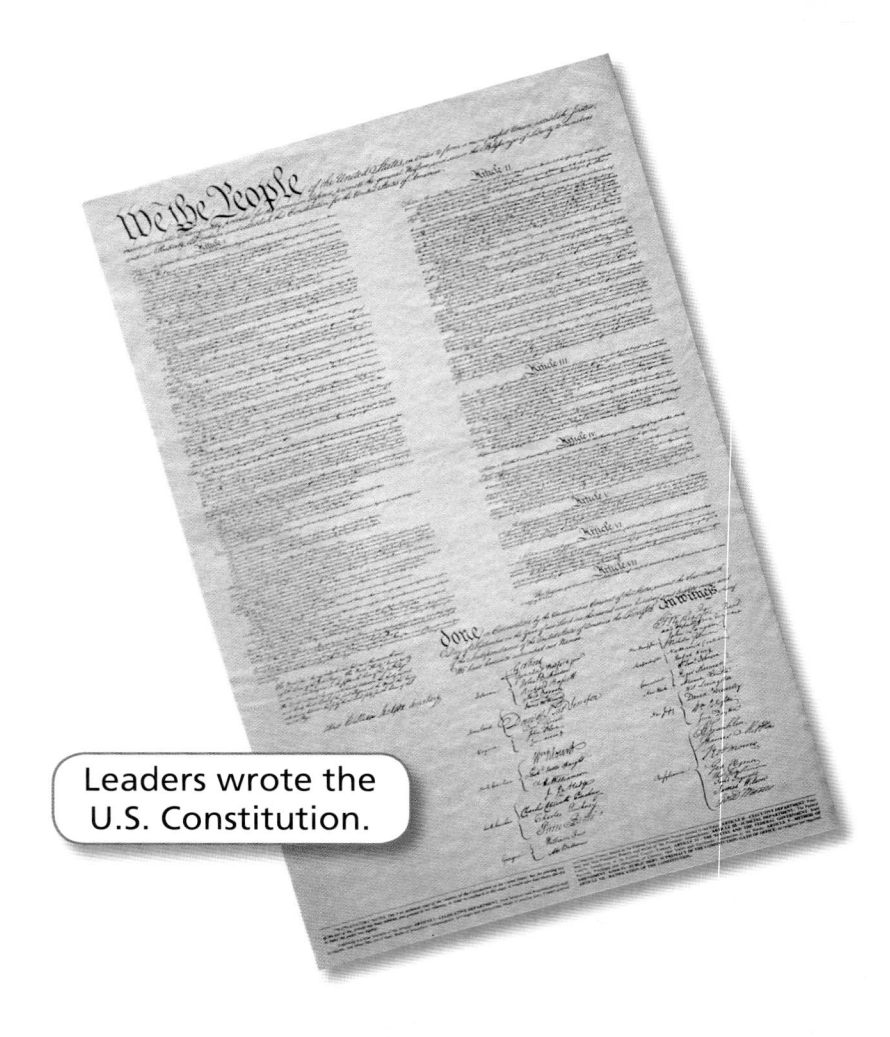

To write the Constitution, leaders had to agree. They did not always agree on laws.

They did agree on one thing. Everybody had to follow the laws. This was important to keep people safe.

The Bill of Rights

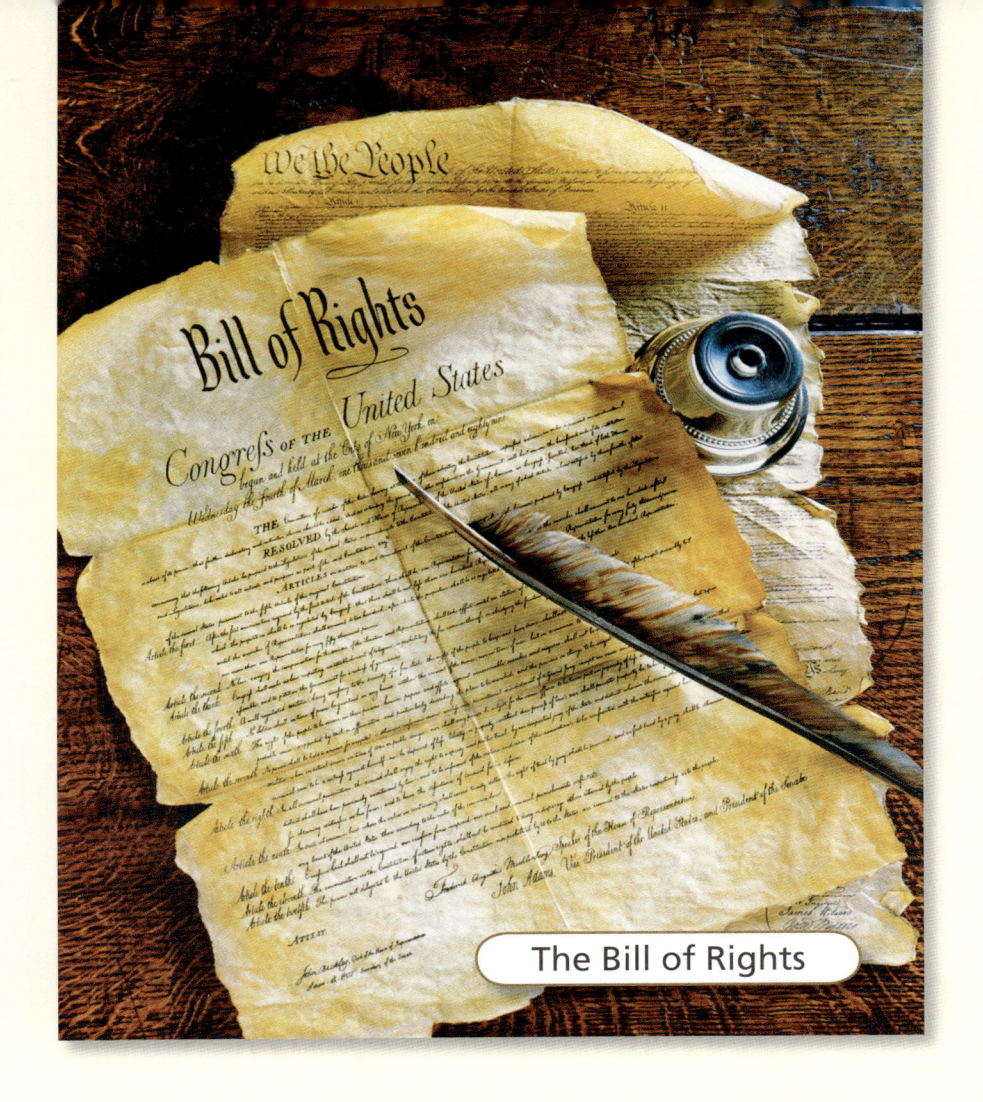

The leaders wanted to protect the rights of people. They did not want their country to have a king again.

So they made a list. This list is called The Bill of Rights. You learned about some of these freedoms, or rights.

Sometimes people want to take these rights away. The Constitution protects these rights. The laws in the Constitution are the most important laws. They protect our freedom.